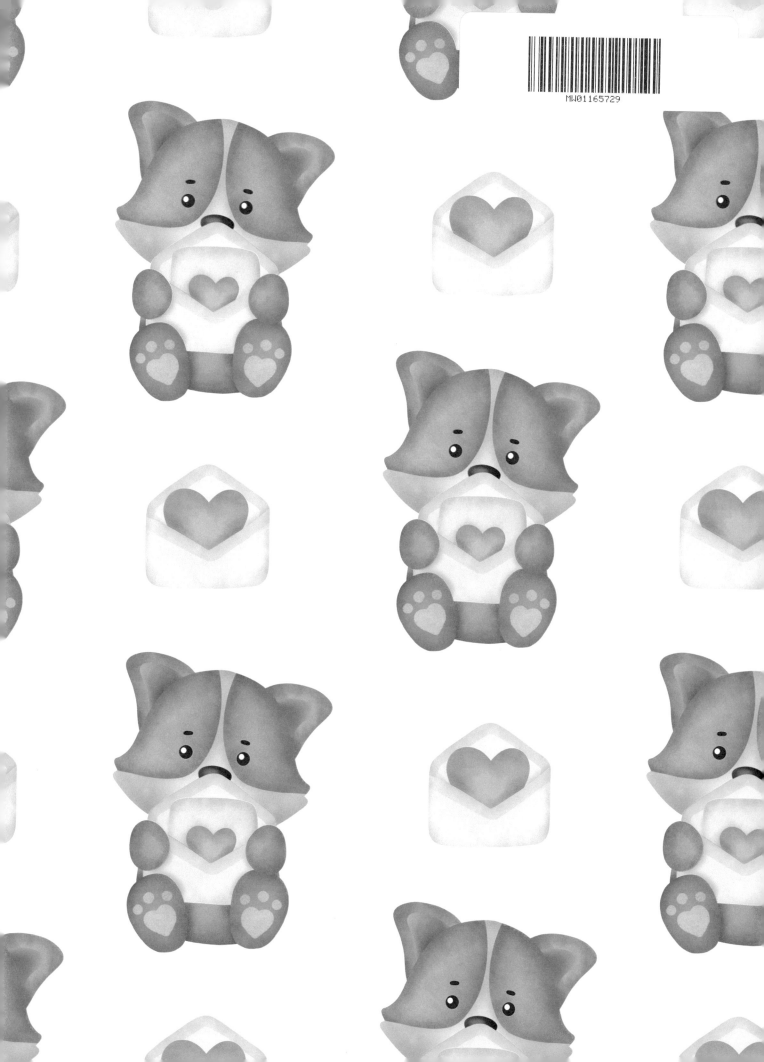

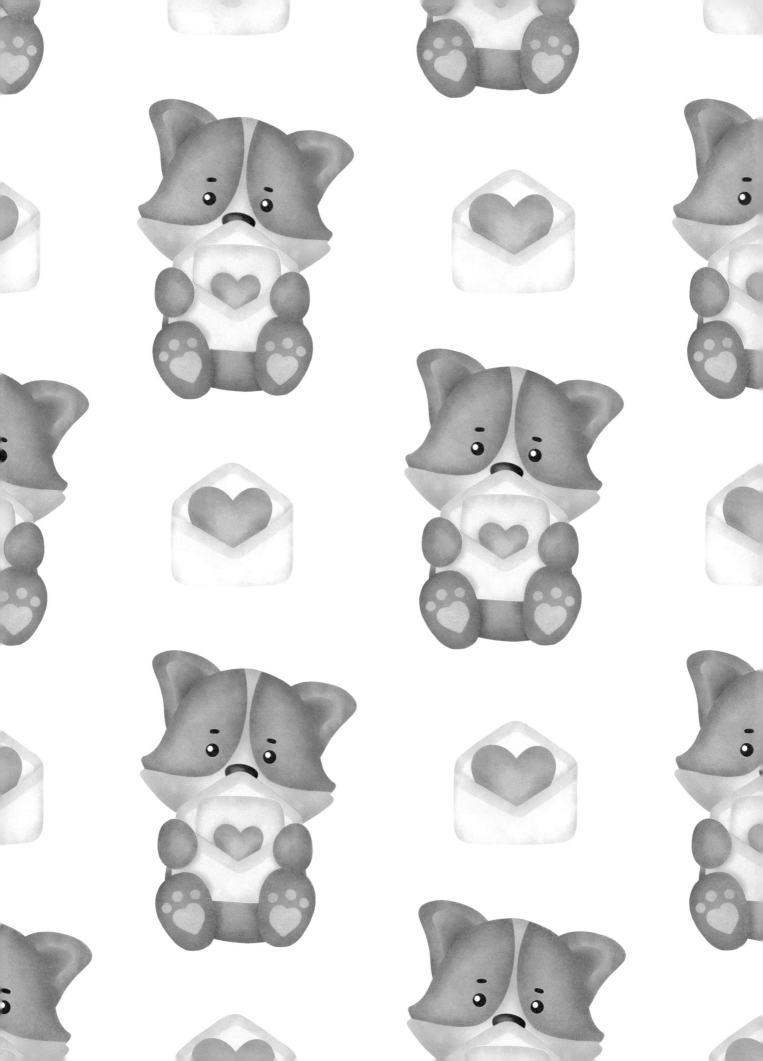

GOD'S LOVE FOR YOU IS LIKE
A HEARTFELT CARD

MADE AND SENT WITH CARE.

HIS LOVE IS LIKE A GREAT BIG HUG

WHILE SAILING ACROSS THE BRIGHT BLUE SKY.

GOD'S LOVE FOR YOU IS LIKE A FRIEND FILLED ROOM

WITH SWEET TREATS TO SHARE.

HIS LOVE FOR YOU IS LIKE A
SWEET BOUQUET OF FRAGRANT FLOWERS

AND BIG RED HEART BALLOONS.

GOD'S PRESENCE BRINGS JOY AND LAUGHTER

THAT FILLS THE AIR.

GOD'S WORDS ARE LIKE A TUMMY FULL OF GRANDMA'S SWEET HOME BAKED TREATS

MADE WITH LOVE AND EXTRA SPECIAL CARE.

HIS LOVE FOR YOU IS A WARM SMILE AFTER A LONG DAY

AN UNCONDITIONAL LOVE.

GOD'S LOVE FOR YOU IS NEVER ENDING

LIKE THE VAST OCEAN SEAS.

GOD'S LOVE IS LIKE A SWEET SONGBIRD'S SONG ABOVE YOUR HEAD

THAT WILL COMFORT YOU
JUST LIKE A LULLABY.

HIS LOVE IS LIKE THE WARMTH OF A CUDDLY HUG FROM SOMEONE YOU LOVE

GOD'S LOVE FOR YOU IS HARD TO IMAGINE LIKE THE MYSTERY OF A UNICORN'S HORN.

GOD'S LOVE IS
THE GIFT OF EACH NEW DAY

AND THE LOVING SACRIFICE THAT GOD HAS MADE.

FOR GOD SO LOVED THE WORLD THAT HE GAVE HIS ONE AND ONLY SON, THAT WHOEVER BELIEVES IN HIM SHALL NOT PERISH BUT HAVE ETERNAL LIFE.

JOHN 3:16

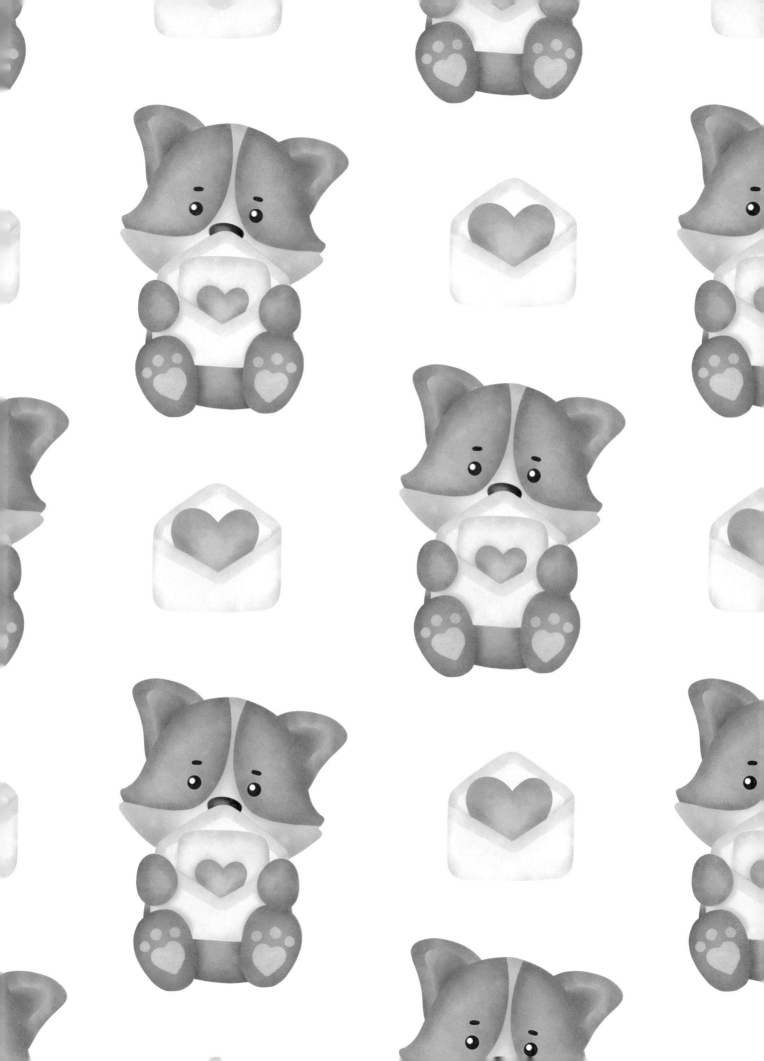

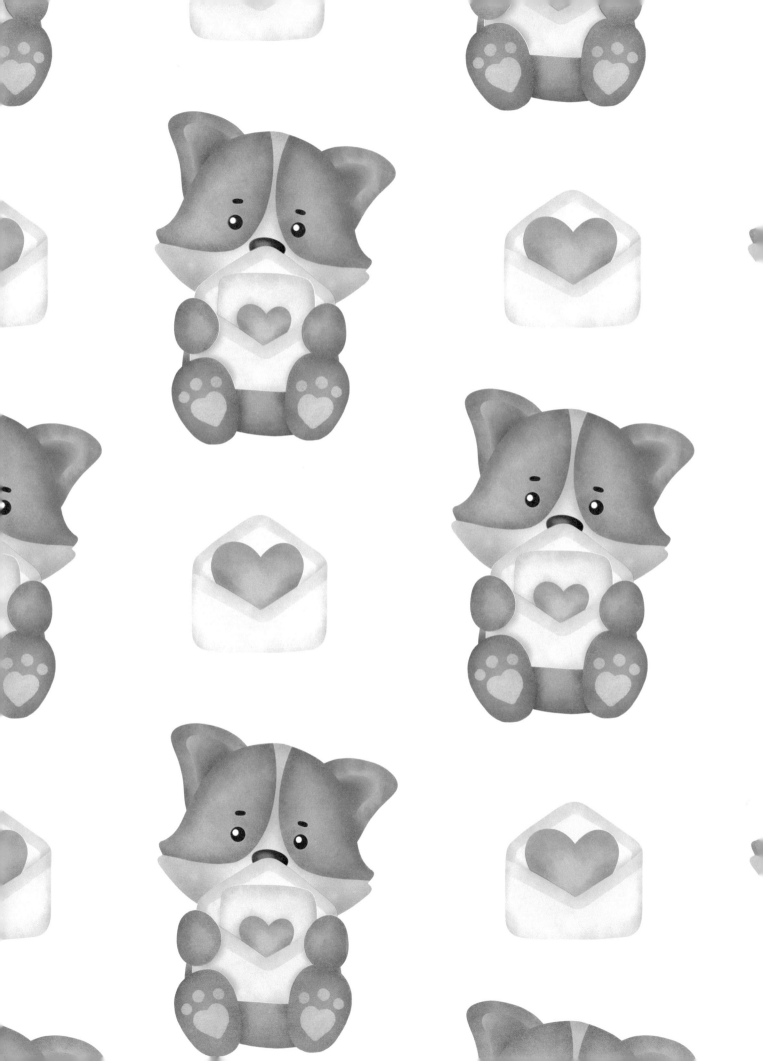

Made in United States
Troutdale, OR
02/10/2025

28848766R00017